Workbook

For

Lindsay C. Gibson's

Adult Children of Emotionally Immature Parents

Smart Reads

Note to readers:
This is an unofficial workbook for Lindsay C. Gibson's
"Adult Children of Emotionally Immature Parents"
designed to enrich your reading experience. The original
book can be purchased on Amazon.

Download Your Free Gift

As a way to say "Thank You" for being a fan of our series, I've included a free gift for you:

Brain Health: How to Nurture and Nourish Your Brain For Top Performance

Go to www.smart-reads.com to get your FREE book.

The Smart Reads Team

Table of Contents

The Purpose of This Book

Why this book?

If you have or grew up with emotionally immature or unavailable parents, this book offers a path to healing from the resulting emotional wounds. The book outlines four types of parents so that the readers can identify and understand their experiences with emotionally immature parents. Also, this book provides strategies to regain control over your life, develop healthier relationships, and break free from the vicious cycle of emotionally immature parents.

Who is this book for?

This book is meant for anybody (adults or children) who has experienced emotional loneliness in their lives. If you have dealt with loneliness due to isolation or detachment from others, feeling like nobody truly understands you, or that internal critical voice that you've obeyed without question, then this book is for you.

This book is essential for anyone who was raised by emotionally immature parents. The reality is that we all bear childhood trauma that we need to heal and be liberated from. If you carry these burdens, this book will be a good read for you.

What's in this workbook and how can it help?

Lindsay Gibson's awesome book (which you should read as well) addresses healing from parents who were distant, rejecting, or self-involved. This workbook summarizes the key lessons from Gibson's book and goes through exercises to recognize and address emotional trauma due to emotionally immature parents. By doing so, you give yourself the best chance to heal from past trauma caused by emotionally immature parents.

What to expect from this book?

We hope that this book will empower you to break free from familiar yet harmful patterns of emotional immaturity. By doing so, you have a chance for genuine freedom and a future free from past hurt and trauma from parents or anyone else. When you understand the past, you can deal with the future.

How To Use This Workbook

This workbook is designed to help you have a deeper understanding of Lindsay Gibson's book. In order to get the most out of the book and apply the concepts, do the following.

1) Read the chapter summary in this book to get an overview and big picture understanding of the book.

2) Read Lindsay Gibson's original work. The details of the book will be easier to understand once you grasp the big picture.

3) Once you understand the core concepts, start working through the exercises in this workbook.

4) To assist you with applying the main concepts, the following exercises are present.

Key Takeaways: Main key points to help you understand the most important topics.

Reflective Questions: These questions guide you to reflect on your own experiences and figure out what needs to be done to change your life. Write your thoughts in the lines present in this workbook.

Action Step: Practical steps are discussed to lead you to take action so you can improve your life.

You must **THINK** before doing. This is how you can make changes to lead a new life.

Overview of *Adult Children of Emotionally Immature Parents: How to Heal from Distant, Rejecting, or Self-Involved Parents*

"Adult Children of Emotionally Immature Parents" talks about how our parents' **emotional immaturity can affect us**. It starts by saying that adults are usually seen as more mature than kids, but that's not always true. Some parents with **poor emotional intelligence** use unhealthy ways to handle their feelings, and they **avoid facing reality**.

These **poor coping skills can really hurt the children** of emotionally immature parents. Emotional neglect in childhood is bad, and it's been an issue for a long time. This book wants to help everyone including adult children (who are now parents) who struggle with emotional immaturity and self-centeredness due to an emotionally immature parent, so they can give themselves and their kids a healthier life.

Topics That Are Covered

The book covers various topics like how emotional maturity differs and why talking to certain family members can be tough and draining. It helps readers **set realistic expectations** and deal with emotionally immature people in a healthy way. It also explains why some parents can't give the emotional connection their children need.

The book has **ten chapters**, covering the following topics:

Chapter 1: Emotionally immature parents often lead to lonely kids.

Chapters 2 and 3: Description of common traits of emotionally immature parents and the problems kids face in these families.

Chapter 4: Exploration of the four types of emotionally immature parents.

Chapter 5: Discussion about people who sacrifice themselves for their families.

Chapter 6: Introduction to the 'internalizer' personality, someone who reflects on their actions a lot.

Chapter 7: Stories of people who broke free from the cycle of emotionally immature parents.

Chapter 8: Explanation of the 'Maturity Awareness Approach,' a way to understand someone's level of functioning.

Chapter 9: More stories of people who used this approach and had positive results.

Chapter 10: Tips to identify kind and emotionally mature people.

The author hopes the book will make readers feel validated and empowered to create a healthier path for themselves, different from the one their emotionally immature parents showed them.

Chapter 1 – How Emotionally Immature Parents Affect Their Adult Children's Lives

Emotional Loneliness

Chapter one discusses "**Emotional Loneliness**", which is feeling disconnected from others due to emotionally immature parents. Even if a child's physical needs are met, emotional support is essential for them to feel secure.

Emotional intimacy means having someone to share feelings with, but **emotional loneliness** happens when there's no one to talk to about emotions. This can lead to unhealthy coping mechanisms and difficulties in relationships later in life.

Recognizing Emotional Loneliness

Recognizing emotional loneliness can guide us towards healthier relationships. Children of emotionally immature parents might struggle to trust their instincts and have lower self-confidence. Understanding the impact of our upbringing can help us heal and break the cycle of emotional loneliness.

The book shares stories of David and Rhonda to explain **emotional loneliness**. David felt isolated growing up, and Rhonda experienced it when her family moved, but she had no one to talk to about her fears.

Feeling emotionally lonely is valid and important. It tells us that something in our relationships needs attention. While adults can use this feeling to improve their future, children might cope with it in less healthy ways.

The cycle of loneliness can repeat throughout adulthood, as we tend to seek what's familiar to us. Recognizing our parent's emotional immaturity is essential to move past this cycle.

The book further illustrates this point through the story of Sophie. She was in a relationship with an emotionally immature boyfriend, and her mother (also emotionally immature) sided with him. Recognizing such patterns of emotional immaturity is crucial for healing.

The Impact of Emotional Loneliness

Feelings of guilt and loneliness are not tied to any gender. Men may show their struggles differently, but both men and women can feel lonely if their parents are emotionally immature.

These feelings can take different forms. Some may feel they need to play a role to feel close to their parents, while others may feel trapped taking care of their parents. Learning to trust our feelings is essential to break free from these patterns.

Lack of self-confidence and difficulty expressing needs are common traits in adults with emotionally immature parents. Childhood loneliness can lead to adult traumas like anxiety, depression, or nightmares.

Emotional intimacy is crucial for well-being. Ancient people relied on emotional closeness for survival, and it still affects us today.

The first chapter reminds us that a lack of emotional intimacy can lead to emotional loneliness, which in turn affects self-confidence, relationships, and well-being. Understanding our parent's emotional loneliness is crucial to healing and breaking the cycle.

Key Points

- Emotional intimacy means having someone you can talk to about your feelings.

- Emotional loneliness occurs whenever there is a lack of emotional intimacy. This can result in various relationship and mental health issues.

- You can feel emotional loneliness even if all your physical needs are being met.

- Use your feelings of emotional loneliness to make changes for a healthier future.

- Healing begins when one learns how their parent's emotional loneliness impacts them.

Reflective Questions

- Do you think your parents were emotionally mature? Why or why not?

_____
_____
_____
_____
_____

- Do any of the symptoms of emotional loneliness resonate with you? If so, which ones?

_____
_____
_____
_____
_____

- Do you have any relationships that make you feel emotional intimacy?

_____
_____
_____
_____
_____

- How do you think your parent's emotional loneliness impacted you?

_____
_____
_____
_____
_____

Action Plan

- Recognize whether your parents were emotionally mature or not when you were a child.

_____
_____
_____
_____
_____

- Think about how your childhood was impacted by your parents' emotional maturity (or lack thereof).

_____
_____
_____
_____
_____

- Accept your feelings of emotional loneliness, and don't feel bad about them. Use your feelings as a starting point for creating a healthier future.

_____
_____
_____
_____
_____

- Start recognizing your parent's emotional loneliness and how this may have impacted you.

_____
_____
_____

Chapter 2 – Recognizing the Emotionally Immature Parent

Chapter 2, "**Recognizing the Emotionally Immature Parent**," aims to help you see your parents objectively. Analyzing them is not disrespectful; it leads to better self-understanding and confidence.

Emotionally immature parents may not realize how their behavior affects their children. This book equips readers with tools to become more self-aware. Remember, your parents don't have to know you're reading this.

Emotional Immaturity Exercise

To understand your parent's emotional immaturity, the author offers an exercise.

Check off statements that apply to your parents.

- Overreact to seemingly minor things

- Lack of empathy or emotional awareness

- Seem uncomfortable dealing with feelings

- Become irritated when viewpoints that differ from theirs are brought up

- Confide in you, but not let you confide in them

- Acted without thinking of others' feeling

- Mainly ignore you unless you were really sick

- Inconsistent

- Became unhelpful, angry, or sarcastic when you were upset

- Talked about themselves and their interests far more than you

- Become defensive at polite disagreements

- Not care about your success

- Refuse to change their opinions even when presented with facts and logic

- Never took responsibility for their part in a problem

- Refuse to entertain new ideas

- If you checked off more than one of the above statements, then you likely had immature parents.

Emotional Regression vs Personality Patterns

Before making any judgments, the book explores two essential topics: **temporary emotional regression** and **personality patterns**. When people are tired or stressed, they might emotionally regress and lose control. However, this differs from personality patterns of emotional immaturity, which involves a repetitive pattern of not considering how one's actions affect others. Emotionally immature individuals don't apologize or feel remorse for their behavior. So, **make sure the traits you observed are consistent patterns** and not just occasional emotional regression before concluding your parents are emotionally immature.

Signs of Emotional Maturity

Another important concept to understand is maturity. It means being able to think objectively and form strong emotional bonds with others. Mature individuals communicate openly, express their needs, and can build their own independent identity. **Signs of emotional maturity** include facing problems directly, using healthy coping strategies, managing emotions, processing feelings, and being honest about weaknesses.

Signs of Emotional Immaturity

On the other hand, signs of emotional immaturity include:

- Inflexibility and close-mindedness
- Low tolerance for stress
- Being guided by emotions
- Subjectivity rather than objectivity
- Lack of respect for others' viewpoints
- Egocentric, self-centered, self-involved, self-preoccupied
- Inability to self-reflect

Emotionally immature individuals often **seek constant attention** and **lack empathy** for others. They may also exhibit **role reversal**, treating their child as if the child is the parent.

Emotional immaturity is illustrated through Freida's story. Her father's emotional immaturity led to physical abuse, and she was expected to comfort him like a child. He sought unconditional approval, even for his abusive behavior. As an adult, Freida had to break free from her father's emotional demands and find her own path.

Freida's experience is not uncommon, raising the question of why there are many emotionally immature parents. The author suggests that **parents who are emotionally immature may have had emotionally immature parents themselves**. Outdated beliefs of children being seen and not heard, along with past acceptance of physical abuse as punishment, contribute to this pattern. Recently, the idea of supporting children's feelings and uniqueness has gained popularity.

The Effects of Emotional Immaturity

Emotional immaturity can have deeper effects, leading to emotional shutdown. This manifests as inconsistent actions, a defense mechanism to avoid feelings, emotional limitations, and a fear of feelings known as "**affect phobia**." It can even impact a person's ability to think conceptually and analyze emotions and ideas.

The chapter concludes with the **recognition that emotional immaturity is not a new issue**. Growing up in an emotionally immature environment can hinder a child's emotional and intellectual development, leading to egocentrism, reactivity, and a lack of objectivity. The next chapter will delve into relationships with emotionally immature parents and the challenges adult children may face in such relationships.

Key Points

- It is not disrespectful to understand your parent's emotional maturity level.

- Personality patterns are typical actions from a person. Temporary emotional regression can occur when someone is very stressed or tired, but it is not their default reaction.

- Emotional mature people can think objectively and are able to build healthy relationships.

- Emotionally immature people shy away from emotions, which can result in dire consequences.

Reflective Questions

- Understand the difference between personality patterns and temporary emotional regression.

_____
_____
_____
_____
_____

- Learn the common traits of emotionally mature people

_____
_____
_____
_____
_____

- Learn the common traits of emotionally immature people

_____

_____

_____

_____

_____

- Understand the deeper effects of emotional immaturity.

_____

_____

_____

_____

_____

Action Plan

- Recognize that evaluating your parent's emotional maturity is not disrespectful but a helpful exercise for yourself.

_____

_____

_____

_____

_____

- Complete the exercise in the chapter. How many boxes did you check?

_____

_____

_____

_____

_____

- Based on the description provided in the chapter on emotionally mature people, do you have any such people in your life?

_____
_____
_____
_____
_____

- Do you think you are emotionally mature? If not, do you want to be?

_____
_____
_____
_____
_____

Chapter 3 – How it Feels to Have a Relationship with an Emotionally Immature Parent

Chapter 3, "How it Feels to Have a Relationship with an Emotionally Immature Parent," explores exactly what the title suggests. The author describes the dynamics of such relationships and how emotionally immature parents fail to meet their children's emotional needs. **Children don't choose their parents**, so having emotionally immature parents can lead to a lifetime of disappointment.

To assess if you had childhood difficulties due to an emotionally immature parent, the author offers an exercise. **Go through the assessment below** and mark any items that apply to your relationship with your parents. It's recommended to take the assessment multiple times, focusing on different parents or step-parents each time.

Childhood Difficulties Exercise

Check off the items that apply to your relationship with your parent:

- You felt ignored, like you never had your parent's full attention

- The whole household was affected by your parent's mood

- Felt like you had to guess what your parents wanted

- Tried harder to understand your parent than they tried to understand you

- Difficult to communicate openly and honestly with parent

- Parents expected people should play roles with no deviations

- Parents did not respect your privacy

- Believe parents thought of you as emotional or too sensitive

- Parents played favorites

- Feelings of guilt and shame were common when you were around your parents

- Apologies from your parents were rare. Parents did not try to resolve situations between you and them

- Feelings of pent-up anger toward your parents that you could not share

After taking the assessment, the chapter delves into specific relationship characteristics.

Traits of Emotionally Immature Parents

Communicating with emotionally immature parents can be difficult, sometimes one-sided, leaving the child feeling shut down. Talking to them may feel like conversing with self-focused children, with frequent interruptions.

Anger is a valid response to having an emotionally immature parent, as shown by John Bowlby's studies on children's feelings when left alone by their parents. These feelings may persist into adulthood, leading to unhealthy coping tactics such as repression, guilt, passive-aggressiveness, depression, and suicide.

Emotional contagion is a common trait of emotionally immature parents, where they act out their emotions instead of expressing them directly. It's similar to a baby crying when hungry because they can't verbalize their needs yet.

Emotional work is rarely done by emotionally immature parents. It involves trying to understand others' emotions and fulfilling their emotional needs, as introduced by Harriet Fraad in the concept of emotional labor. Emotionally mature individuals can perform emotional labor, but emotionally immature people struggle with it.

Emotionally immature people have poor receptive capacity and may seek sympathy for their feelings but reject help or suggestions to resolve their issues. They often resist attempts to show care and support.

Emotionally immature people avoid repairing relationships when issues arise. Instead, they shift blame to others for not forgiving quickly, even if they caused the problem. They expect things to go back to normal immediately, disregarding the need for the other person to process emotions and rebuild trust.

Demand mirroring is a skill lacking in many emotionally immature individuals. It involves reflecting the other person's emotions on your face to convey understanding. Emotionally mature parents model this behavior for their children to learn, but emotionally immature parents demand their children to mirror them, even if the child doesn't know how.

Emotionally immature parents tie their self-esteem to their children's compliance. They may feel inadequate if they can't instantly soothe their children. An example of this is illustrated through Jeff's story, where his father becomes angry and insults him when Jeff struggles with homework, rather than finding a better way to explain the material.

Emotionally immature parents hold sacred roles for their children and expect them to fit specific molds, simplifying the parent's life. They believe their authority allows them to do as they please, and they may use coercion, guilt, or shame to enforce these roles.

The final traits of emotionally immature individuals mentioned in this chapter are **enmeshment, playing favorites, and an inconsistent sense of time**. Enmeshment involves sacrificing one's emotional needs for another's sake. Playing favorites may lead a parent to prefer one child or even someone outside the family over their own child. Emotionally immature people struggle to predict their emotions, resulting in an inconsistent sense of time and an inability to learn from the past.

Emotionally immature individuals are **rarely accountable for their actions**. They lack a strong sense of self, making communication difficult, and they rely on enmeshment instead of emotional intimacy, allowing anxieties to overpower authentic relationships. In the next chapter, the author explores early mother-child attachments and their role in forming immature characteristics. Additionally, chapter four introduces the four main types of emotionally immature parents.

Key Points

- You do not get to choose your parents, so feeling disappointed at their lack of emotional maturity is valid.

- An equally valid emotion is feeling anger at not receiving emotional intimacy from your parents.

- Lack of emotional maturity can take many different forms in a relationship.

- Emotionally immature people let their anxieties supersede authentic relationships.

Reflective Questions

- How does your parent's emotional immaturity make you feel?

_____
_____
_____
_____
_____

- Have you accepted these emotions? Why or why not?

_____
_____

_____
_____
_____

- How many of the boxes in the exercise did you check?

_____
_____
_____
_____
_____

- How does your parent's emotional immaturity impact your relationship with them?

_____
_____
_____
_____
_____

- What do you wish was different about your relationship with your parents?

_____
_____
_____
_____
_____

Action Plan

- Accept any negative feelings you may have about your parent's emotional immaturity.

_____
_____
_____
_____
_____

- Take the assessment for each of the parental figures in your life.

_____
_____
_____
_____
_____

- Understand the common symptoms of emotional immaturity in a relationship.

_____
_____
_____
_____
_____

- Recognize how your parents' emotional immaturity impacts your relationship with them.

_____
_____
_____
_____
_____

Chapter 4 – Four Main Types of Emotionally Immature Parents

Chapter four, **four main types of emotionally immature parents**, dives into the four categories of emotionally immature parents. While each type is different, the author notes that emotionally immature parents make their children feel lonely. No matter the type of emotionally immature parent, there are a few shared characteristics: **self-involvement, narcissism, egocentricity, and insensitivity**. Children of such parents often feel "de-selfed," a term coined by Bowen in 1978. This feeling occurs because the parent's needs overshadow the child.

The author references a study conducted by Mary Ainsworth, Sylvia Bell, and Donelda Stayton. This study found four dimensions regarding a mother's behavior toward her children. These dimensions are:

- Sensitivity-insensitivity
- Acceptance-interference
- Cooperation- interference
- Accessible-ignoring

The study found that mothers with a **high degree of sensitivity also had high acceptance, cooperation, and accessibility**. These sensitive mothers had a secure attachment to their infants. On the other hand, insensitive mothers had an insecure attachment to their children. These mothers were unaware of their baby's behavior, did not understand their child's behavior, and could not empathize with their infant. These mothers do not have helpful and comforting reactions to their baby's behavior, or their reactions are too late.

Building from this study, the author defines **four emotional types of immature parents**. These types are:

1. Emotional parent

2. Driven parent

3. Passive parent

4. Rejecting parent

The Emotional Parent

Parents who are emotional are easily upset can be considered very infant-like. The rest of the family works to soothe them rather than them taking responsibility for their own emotions. These parents can make their children feel like they are constantly in a delicate situation. In extreme situations, the author notes that these parents may have mental illnesses such as bipolar, narcissism, or borderline personality disorder (BPD). At times, emotional parents may even threaten suicide. This parenting type is characterized by emotional insecurity, low self-control, and limited stress tolerance.

The Driven Parent

Unlike an emotional parent, **a driven parent looks average to the outsider**. In some cases, these parents can seem very invested in their children. But these parents focus on getting things done. Children of such parents have trouble building initiative and self-control. While driven parents may be hardworking, their single-minded focus means their children often become depressed and unmotivated. At their core, these parents expect their children to want the same things they do. So they drive their children to these goals without considering the child's wants and needs. Driven parents want their children to succeed, but this desire outweighs the parent's ability to support the child unconditionally.

The Passive Parent

Passive parents often choose very dominant partners and acquiesce to their partner's wishes. This parenting type is usually emotionally available. Until things get too intense, then they retreat. These parents are often playful and relaxed but use their children to meet their own emotional needs. This reliance on the child for emotional needs can even make the child feel sexualized. Passive parents are not someone a child can turn to for help. Emotional needs are entirely one-sided. While these parents can be described as nice, they are not responsible.

The Rejecting Parent

The final emotionally immature parent type is the **rejecting parent**. These parents are often alone. When their child tries to be close to them, this type of parent often rejects the child's attempts. To the child, this rejection feels like an emotional door slammed into the face. A common archetype of this parent is a daunting and aloof father. The whole family walks around on tiptoes to avoid upsetting them. Growing up in such households, children can think of themselves as a burden. As an adult, children of rejecting parents find it hard ask for or express their needs.

The author includes an exercise in the book to determine your parent's type. Read through the following statements about parents and check off the ones that apply to yours. Then, tally up your check marks and see which parenting type gets the most checks.

Parent Type Exercise

Emotional parent

- Focuses on own needs

- Little empathy

- Disrespectful of boundaries

- Talks about themselves a lot

- Does not self-reflect

- Rarely tries to repair the relationship

- Reactive

- Closed off or distant

- Emotions are often displayed in frightening ways

- Expects the child to soothe them, but does not soother child

- Often sees themself as the victim

Driven parent

- Focuses on their own needs

- Little empathy

- Disrespects boundaries

- No reciprocal communication

- No self-reflection

- Reactive

- Overly goal-oriented

- Always in charge

- Always tries to fix things, even when not needed or wanted

- Rigid values

- Perfectionist

Passive parent

- Preoccupied with own needs

- Little to no empathy

- Enmeshed

- Emotionally intimate at times

- Minimal reciprocal communication

- No self-reflection

- Does not repair a relationship

- Can be thoughtful

- Kind, but not protective

- Too laid back

- Affectionate, but doe snot support child

- Is scared of being the bad guy

- Considers themselves relaxed and easy-going

Rejecting parent

- Focuses on own needs

- Lacks empathy

- Strict boundaries

- Disconnected

- Hostile at times

- Rarely engages in communication

- Can be combative or demeaning

- Overly distant

- Ignore child

- Is often angry at a child

- Sees the child as a burden

- Uses mockery and dismissiveness

No matter the type of emotionally immature parent, these parents are insensitive and emotionally unavailable. They lack empathy and are difficult to communicate with. Children of such parents do not feel emotionally seen. While emotionally immature parents fall into one of the four categories described in this chapter, children of these parents typically develop one of two main coping strategies. The next chapter focuses on these coping mechanisms.

Key Points

- All emotionally immature parents cause their children to feel lonely.

- There are four dimensions to the mother-child relationship

- Emotional parents let their feelings control their actions.

- Driven parents let their own goals control their actions.

- Passive parents let their emotional needs control their actions.

- Rejecting parents lets their fear of emotions control their actions.

Reflective Questions

- Did you often feel lonely in your childhood?

  _____

  _____

  _____

  _____

  _____

- What are the four dimensions of the mother-child relationship?

  _____

  _____

  _____

  _____

  _____

- What are the four types of emotionally immature parents?

  _____

  _____

  _____

  _____

  _____

- Which type of parent do you think you had?

  _____

  _____

  _____

  _____

  _____

Action Plan

- Reflect on the emotions you often had in childhood.

_____
_____
_____
_____
_____

- Understand the four types of emotionally immature parents

_____
_____
_____
_____
_____

- Take the assessment included in the chapter.

_____
_____
_____
_____
_____

- Identify which type of parent you had. You can take the assessment multiple times for different parents or step-parents.

_____
_____
_____

Chapter 5 – How Different Children React to Emotionally Immature Parenting

Chapter 5, How Different Children React to Emotionally Immature Parenting, dives into the two coping styles children of emotionally immature parents develop. The author notes that neither coping style is healthy for children. Both styles prevent children from developing to their full potential. Children of emotionally immature parents are forced to put their own wants, needs, and desires to the side to keep the peace. As adults, these children often begin to find themselves again, which the author covers in detail in chapter seven.

Coping Styles As Children: Healing Fantasies and Role-Self

This chapter discusses **healing fantasies**. Healing fantasies are a story of how life will look when we are truly happy. Children of emotionally immature parents try to change themselves and others to fit this narrative. Regardless of the specifics, healing fantasies always have the same theme, feeling loved and attended. These fantasies can affect adult relationships. If the fantasy is not met, adults can feel let down or angry with their partner or friends.

Another concept the chapter introduces is **role-self**. A role-self occurs when children learn acting a certain way gets their parent's attention. This can include acting out or behaving in a way the parents desire.

Healing Fantasy and Role-Self Exercise

To uncover your healing fantasy and role-self, the author includes an exercise. To complete this exercise, you'll need two sheets of paper. On one sheet, write "**healing fantasy**" across the top. On the other sheet, write "**role-self**."

On the healing fantasy page, complete these statements:

I desire people to be more _____.

I don't understand why it is so hard for people to _____.

I want to be treated _____.

I want to find someone who will _____.

In my ideal world, other people are _____.

On the Role-Self page, finish these sentences

I work really hard to be _____.

People like me because _____.

No one notices how much I _____.

No one does _____. I always have to do that.

I work to be _____ kind of person.

At the bottom of both pages, create a summary of your responses. You now know your healing fantasy and role-self based on the summary you created. Next, ask yourself if you want to keep living following these roles and fantasies or do you want to be authentic.

Coping Strategies As Adults: Internalizers and Externalizers

After the exercise, the author introduces the two coping styles of people with emotionally immature parents: internalizers and externalizers. Internalizers are deep thinkers who try to solve problems by themselves. They are often self-sacrificing and feel guilty when they make others unhappy.

Externalizers act before thinking. They use constant trial and error, but they don't remember lessons learned from the trial and error. Externalizers often fall into a continual cycle of self-defeat. They look to others for solutions rather than trying to fix their own life. However, there is a continuum of externalizers. Some act more like internalizers, while others externalize to the extreme. This extreme can even result in sibling abuse.

The author emphasizes that the externalizer and internalizer coping strategies can be mixed. Externalizers can often become more internalizing. Alternatively, internalizers can become externalizers when in high-stress situations. However, externalizers tend to seek treatment due to the potential for extreme nature.

Internalizer/Externalizer Assessment

The author includes an exercise to identify your own coping style. It can be downloaded from http://www.newharbinger.com/31700 and is also summarized below. Check off the boxes that sound like something you would do:

Externalizer traits:

- Live in the present

- Look for outside solutions

- Act now. Think later

- Underestimate difficulties

- React quickly

- Blame problems and circumstances on others

- Involve yourself in other's problems

- Escape reality in order to feel better

- Impulsive

- Anger easily

- Rarely self-reflect

- Often monopolize conversations

Internalizer traits:

- Worry about the future

- Look internally for solutions

- Always try to improve situations

- Overestimate difficulties

- Self-reflect

- Problem-solve on your own

- Often feel guilty

- Put others' needs before your own

- Think before acting

- Easily confront reality

Whatever your coping style, finding balance is essential. Extreme internalizers and extreme externalizers do not handle situations in a healthy manner. But, externalizers tend to have a harder time developing healthy skills than internalizers. Ultimately, internalizers think all solutions come from themself, whereas externalizers think all solutions come from others. Neither is a healthy solution for all scenarios. In the next chapter, the author dives into more details of internalizers to help them find their true self.

Key Points

- Healing fantasies are the stories children of emotionally immature parents create of life when they feel loved.

- Role-self is the identity children create to receive attention from their parents.

- Internalizing is a coping strategy that involves looking within for answers.

- Externalizing is a coping strategy that involves looking to others for answers.

- Finding a balance of coping mechanisms is critical to being a healthy adult.

Reflective Questions

- How do healing fantasies and role-self differ?

_____

_____

_____

_____

_____

- What is an internalizer coping strategy?

_____

_____

_____

_____

_____

- What is an externalizer coping strategy?

_____

_____

_____

_____

_____

- What coping strategy do you use more?

_____

_____

_____

_____

_____

Action Plan

- Take the role-self and healing fantasy assessment

_____
_____
_____
_____
_____

- Understand your healing fantasy.

_____
_____
_____
_____
_____

- Identify your role-self.

_____
_____
_____
_____
_____

- Use the internalizer/externalizer assessment to learn your coping mechanism.

_____
_____
_____
_____
_____

- Do you want to find more balance in your coping mechanism?

_____

_____

_____

_____

_____

Chapter 6 – What It's Like to Be an Internalizer

Internalizers are sensitive and perceptive individuals. They have a deep need for connection and a tendency to neglect their own needs. This can lead to potential resentment and exhaustion in their relationships.

Chapter 6, What It's Like to Be an Internalizer, dives deeper into the internal world of internalizers. As children, internalizers are more aware than their peers. They recognize when a parent is not truly connecting with them. This can cause more pain and loneliness than it would for less perceptive children. Chapter 6 focuses on these feelings by breaking down the common characteristics and pitfalls of internalizers.

Internalizers are very sensitive and perceptive. They can be described as an emotional tuning fork. This attunement can happen very early in childhood. A 2013 study by Conradt, Measelle, and Ablow found children as young as five months old can be in tune with their caretaker's moods.

Due to their sensitive nature, **internalizers can have very strong emotions**. Their emotions easily show on their face. For emotion-phobic parents, this is especially alarming and causes the parent to disengage when the child needs support the most. This causes the child to feel immense pain in not sharing their emotions. Internalizers have a deep need for connection. However, they may rarely get the opportunity to share their emotional experience.

Another common trait of internalizers is the **need for genuine engagement**. This need is not limited to humans. A 2011 study by Stephen Porges found mammals of all types are calmed by being around one another. For humans, this genuine engagement can be found with people both inside and outside the family.

While internalizers want to engage deeply with others, **they dislike taking help from others**. The author gives a classic example of an internalizer apologizing for crying in a therapist's office, even though a therapist's office is a very appropriate place to cry.

Internalizers rarely make their needs known, making them susceptible to neglect. By hiding their own needs, internalizers don't receive the help and care they need from others. This is especially true when parents are self-involved and unable to realize what their children need.

Because they are often neglected, **internalizers function on limited recognition**. Their emotional needs are neglected by others, so internalizing children learn to ignore their own feelings. When they do express their needs, they only receive very basic, superficial support back, perpetuating the cycle. Furthermore, since internalizers like to solve problems on their own, they are hesitant to label how they are treated as abuse, even with the term is accurate.

In relationships, internalizers put in more work than the other person. As children, they do emotional work for their parents. As adults, they carry all the weight of their romantic and platonic relationships. This is especially unfortunate because people with high emotional needs are often attracted to internalizers. Sadly, many internalizers think that if they neglect their own needs enough, eventually, the other person will give them the love they need and deserve.

The chapter ends with the reminder that internalizers are very sensitive and perspective. They need to relate to others but do not have anyone to relate to in childhood. As adults, **internalizers grow up to have unhealthy ideas about relationships**, putting others before themself. Ultimately, this can result in resentment and exhaustion.

Key Points

- Internalizers are more aware of others' emotions, even at a young age.

- Internalizers' emotional needs are not met by their parents

- As an adult, internalizers can have unhealthy views of relationships.

- These unhealthy views can result in resentment and exhaustion.

Reflective Questions

- After reading this chapter, do you think you are an internalizer? Why or why not?

_____
_____
_____
_____
_____

- What internalizer traits did you recognize in yourself?

_____
_____
_____
_____
_____

- Do you often find yourself pouring energy and time into a relationship but not getting anything back?

_____
_____
_____
_____
_____

- Do you feel resentment or exhaustion in any of your current relationships?

_____
_____
_____
_____
_____

Action Plan

- Understand the common traits of internalizers.

_____
_____
_____

_____

_____

- Recognize the internalizer traits you may have.

_____

_____

_____

_____

_____

- Don't be afraid to express your emotional needs.

_____

_____

_____

_____

_____

- Identify abuse or neglect in your relationships so you can make changes to find healthier relationships.

_____

_____

_____

_____

_____

- Consider what needs to change if you feel resentment or exhaustion in a relationship.

_____

_____

_____

Chapter 7 – Breaking Down and Awakening

The seventh chapter in the book is titled "Breaking Down and Awakening." In this chapter, the author discusses the **process of awakening, when someone realizes they have been playing a role**. The author notes that often, this awakening can cause a breakdown as the person comes to terms with their past and emotions. This breakdown can have symptoms like depression, anxiety, tension, and trouble sleeping.

True Self

Before jumping into this awakening, the author introduces the **"true self ."** This idea can be found even in ancient times when the idea of a soul was first conceived. This true self is part of a person, but it is held back from the outside world. Some other names for this true self are the real self and the core self. The goal of anyone's true self is to optimize energy and functioning.

The desires of your **true self are often like the wants of a child**. Namely, growth, kindness, self-expression, and self-actualization. Children are born in alignment with their true selves. But if they are not supported, this true self is silenced as the child seeks emotional intimacy with their parents by creating a following **role-self**.

To determine your true self, the author includes an exercise. To complete this exercise, gather a pen and a piece of paper. Fold the paper in half lengthwise so only half the page is visible at a time. On one half, write "My True Self," and on the other, write "My Role-Self." Then, fold the page to the "My True Self" side and consider the following topics and questions:

True Self and Role-Self Exercise

- Who were you as a child before you tried to make others happy?

- What did you enjoy doing most as a child?

- What made you feel good as a child?

- If you did not have to worry about money, what would your life look like?

- If you did not have to worry about others, what would you do?

- What were your interests as a child?

- Who were your favorite people when you were growing up? Why"

- Describe your ideal day.

- What makes you feel energized?

- If you had free time, how would you want to spend it?

Next, flip the page over to the "My Role-Self" side and consider the following topics and questions:

- Have you had to change yourself to be admired and respected by those around you?

- Do you do things that do not really interest you?

- What do you do because you think you have to in order to be a good person?

- Are there people in your life who make you feel drained?

- Do you feel bored often? If so, what makes you feel bored?

- How would you describe the role you play in your social circle?

- How do you want others to see you?

- Do you think you are hiding parts of yourself from those around you?

After completing the exercise, don't look at your response right away. Instead, the author recommends waiting a day before returning to your page. Then, consider this question:

Are you living more like your true self or more like your role-self?

In order to live according to your true self, you must first break down your role-self. This breakdown happens when the pain of living according to your role-self outweighs any benefits. As psychologist Jean Piaget discovered in 1963, people must break down their existing mental patterns before they can begin to build new ones.

A breakdown can manifest itself in many ways. Some, like the author's patient Victoria, may begin to experience **panic attacks**. But, Victoria was able to use her breakdown for healing when she sought help and realized her panic attacks were due to living according to her role-self. As Victoria let go of her role-self and began to live more authentically, the panic attacks subsided.

Others may experience a breakdown in the form of **depression**. This was the case for Tilde, one of the author's patients. Tilde felt grateful that her single mother fed and supported her. But she never received emotional intimacy from her mother. This caused Tilde to feel alone, but she felt guilty about these feelings. This compounded into depression. As Tilde began to accept her feelings and create boundaries with her mother, her depression subsided.

Anger is a common response to waking up your true self. This anger can be used as a driver to change things in your life for the better. Others, particularly internalizers, may begin to develop better self-care practices after a breakdown. Creating healthier relationships is another positive outcome after a breakdown. By letting go of our role-self, we can shed unhealthy relationships and build more authentic ones. This can also help us from idealizing others as we see our own worth.

The Benefits Of A Breakdown

After a breakdown, other **positive outcomes** include realizing our strengths, developing new values, and letting go of childhood issues. Each of these outcomes takes time, patience, and self-reflection. But the opportunity of awakening your true self is well worth the effort.

The chapter ends with a reminder that a breakdown is inevitable if we ignore our true selves for too long. This can manifest as panic attacks, depression, anxiety, or sleeplessness. But, by processing your feelings and reflecting on them, it is possible to stop living according to a role-self and live authentically based on your true self.

Key Points

- The role-self is how you act. The true self is who you really are.

- If you ignore your true self for too long, a breakdown is imminent.

- A breakdown can have positive or negative outcomes.

- To live a healthier life, use a breakdown to self-reflect and reshape your life according to your true-self

Reflective Questions

- How is a true self different from a role-self?

_____
_____
_____
_____
_____

- Do you think you are living according to a role-self or true self?

_____
_____
_____
_____
_____

- Have you had any symptoms of a breakdown?

_____
_____
_____
_____
_____

- Do you want to live according to your true self?

_____
_____
_____
_____
_____

Action Plan

- Take the assessment provided in the chapter to determine your true self and role-self.

_____
_____
_____
_____
_____

- Decide if you want to live according to your true self or role-self.

_____
_____
_____
_____
_____

- Identify if you have ever had a breakdown due to ignoring your true self.

_____
_____
_____
_____
_____

- Process and feelings you may have about your role-self. Your feelings are valid.

_____
_____
_____
_____
_____

- Talk to a professional if it would help you process your feelings.

_____
_____
_____
_____
_____

Chapter 8 – How to Avoid Getting Hooked by an Emotionally Immature Parent

The eighth chapter of the book is titled "How to Avoid Getting Hooked by an Emotionally Immature Parent." The chapter begins with acknowledging that, as children, **we think our parents are capable of anything**. So it can be alarming when parents do not provide the love and support children desire. This is further compounded by some of the cultural beliefs surrounding parents. These beliefs may include:

- Every parent loves their child.

- Children can always trust their parents.

- A parent will always be there for their child.

- Children can tell their parents anything.

- Parents love their children unconditionally.

- Adult children can always return home.

- Parents always have your best interests in mind.

- Parents are more knowledgeable than children.

- Parents always act according to their children's best interests.

However, **emotionally immature parents rarely live up to all these expectations**. This chapter dives into these assumptions about parents to help you see your parents more **accurately**. Additionally, the chapter provides tools for communicating with parents to avoid setting themselves up for disappointment. Lastly, the chapter gives a blueprint for honoring your feelings and individuality when talking with your parents.

Recognize False Assumptions About Parents

The **first false assumption** many people have about their parents is that the **parent will change**. The author uses the story of Annie to illustrate this point. Annie was exhausted from a lifetime of one-sided communication with her mother. Annie kept trying to connect, but for her emotion-phobic mother, this connection was alarming. The author coached Annie through realizing that Annie was too focused on her mother's approval and not focused enough on her happiness. Annie's mother would never change. It was up to Annie to find a healthier, more limited relationship with her mother.

Relatedness vs Relationships

The author notes that **detached observation** is the first step in changing your relationship with your parent. Detached observation begins when you become observational. This is the process of operating with a calm perspective rather than reacting from emotion. Think of yourself as a scientist, observing the situation with no emotion.

By staying in a state of observation, you will be able to recognize the differences between relatedness and relationships. **Relatedness** is communication with no emotional exchange. **Relationships** involve creating emotional reciprocity. When talking to an emotionally immature parent, it is **best to aim for relatedness** rather than relationship. This sets realistic expectations when dealing with parents to avoid being let down.

Maturity Awareness Approach

After illustrating the difference between relatedness and relationships, the author introduces the Maturity Awareness Approach. This approach is divided into **three steps** and is used to effectively communicate with emotionally immature people without being disappointed. The three steps in this approach are:

1. **Express yourself. Then let go.** Let the other person know what you want or need, but don't expect them to change. Get your feelings off your chest so you can let them go.

2. **Focus on the outcome, not on the relationship.** Focus on what you want from the conversation, not what you want from the relationship.

3. **Manage. Don't Engage.** Steer the conversation to topics you want to discuss and keep the conversation to a duration that makes you comfortable. Be persistent as you set boundaries, but do not engage in the other person's emotional immaturity.

The rest of the chapter focuses on common concerns regarding the Maturity Awareness Approach. The common concerns and the author's response are summarized in the table below.

Concern	Response
This sounds like a clinical way of talking to my parents. I don't want to feel like an analytical scientist whenever I talk to them.	If you are happy with your relationship with your parents, there is no reason to use this method. However, if you feel angry or disappointed with your parents, this method can help.
I don't want to be closed off from my parents.	You don't have to be distant. Just use this method to avoid being sucked into your parent's drama.
It sounds really hard not to be emotional around my parents.	Emotional contagion occurs when you get wrapped up in another person's emotions. But if you can avoid this emotional contagion, you'll feel much more relaxed.
My parents took good care of me when I was a child. I don't want to be disrespectful to them as an adult.	Your parents are humans. Respect all that they have done for you while also recognizing their limitations.
My parents make me feel guilty. How do I stay	Focus on your breathing to center yourself. Observe

calm?	the facts about the situations to calm yourself and stay analytical.

After addressing these common concerns, the author discusses **stepping out of an old role-self**. Stepping out of your role-self involves letting go of who you have become to meet relational expectations. This involves staying analytical by processing your own thoughts and emotions. Then, be hesitant about any new openness your parents show. It is likely, not genuine and only there to reel you back in.

The chapter ends with a reminder that we rely on our parents from a young age. It can be hard to reevaluate these roles as an adult. However, by using the maturity awareness approach, conversations with emotionally immature parents can be less stressful and anxiety-inducing. By **trying to relate to your parents** instead of building a relationship with them, you can have healthier and more productive interactions with your parents. In the next chapter, the author breaks down common parents between parents and children and provides methods for ending these harmful patterns.

Key Points

- Many children think their parents are capable of anything.

- It is disheartening and alarming when parents show they cannot provide the love and support children need.

- The Maturity Awareness Approach can be used to deal with emotionally immature parents.

- Leave your role-self behind so you can be authentic.

- Be cautious of any new openness your parents show. It is likely an act to suck you back into a one-sided relationship with them.

Reflective Questions

- What are the three steps of the Maturity Awareness Approach?

_____

_____

_____

_____

_____

- How is a relationship different from relatedness?

_____

_____

_____

_____

_____

- Did you have any concerns with this approach? Did the author address them?

_____

_____

_____

_____

_____

- How will you stay calm and thoughtful when interacting with your parents?

_____
_____
_____
_____
_____

- What are some goals you have when talking to your parents?

_____
_____
_____
_____
_____

Action Plan

- Release your expectations of your parents.

_____
_____
_____
_____
_____

- Practice detached observation when interacting with your parents.

_____
_____
_____

_____

_____

- Express yourself to your parents without expecting anything back.

_____

_____

_____

_____

_____

- Choose an outcome when interacting with your parents. Focus on this, not on your relationship with them.

_____

_____

_____

_____

_____

- When talking to your parents, maintain boundaries to discuss topics that make you comfortable.

_____

_____

_____

_____

_____

Chapter 9 – How It Feels to Live Free of Roles and Fantasies

The book's ninth chapter is titled "How It Feels to Live Free of Roles and Fantasies." In this chapter, the author does just that. The author notes that freeing yourself of these roles and fantasies can be difficult, but the relief at the end is well worth the work.

Letting Go of Harmful Dynamics

Before getting into the details, the author reminds readers that **family dynamics greatly impact the roles one plays**. Some of these dynamics include:

- Being discouraged from being yourself

- Being denied your unique needs and preferences

- Doing what you think your parents expect, even as an adult.

However, the author wants you to **release these harmful dynamics** and instead embrace who you are, flaws and all! The author tells the story of Jason, who struggled with a negative and perfectionistic internal monologue. Through therapy, Jason learned that his parents installed this harmful monologue in him. When Jason began to think about his needs and wants, he created a healthier internal monologue that supported him rather than harmed him.

Process Thoughts and Emotions Authentically

As you release yourself from your parents' expectations, you can become in tune with your thoughts and emotions again. If you had emotionally immature parents, your feelings likely frightened them. As a child, you probably learned to hide how you were feeling. But it's important to note that we do not always have control of our thoughts and emotions. Instead, **processing how you think and feel so you can act authentically** is an important skill to learn.

Break Free and Set Boundaries

Breaking free from your parent's expectations allows you to **set boundaries** and choose how much you want to be involved with them. Limiting contact with your parents can be a difficult decision, with much guilt associated with it. This is especially true for internalizers who believe their relationship with their parents will improve if they try harder or do something different. However, limiting contact with people who emotionally drain you is always a healthy decision.

Another positive outcome of setting boundaries with your parents is **increased self-compassion**. Accept your own emotions and give yourself some grace to have a secure sense of self. This can also allow you to step back from other people's issues and not feel weighed down by their problems.

If you had an emotionally immature parent, you might have felt helpless as a child. If you don't receive attention from your parents, it can feel like your desires do not matter. But, by taking some space from your parents and releasing this harmful dynamic, **you can be free to act how you want and to express what you truly feel**.

Build Healthy Relationships

Lastly, ending the harmful dynamics between you and your parents means you are **free to approach relationships on your terms** and free to not want anything from your parents. This can allow you to build healthier adult relationships and rely on the dependable people in your life rather than your emotionally immature parents.

The chapter ends with a reminder that breaking down family dynamics is difficult. But, by putting in the work to do so, it is possible to live a freer and more authentic life. The next and final chapter of the book revisits the emotional maturity method and how it can be used to find emotionally mature people and build fulfilling relationships with them.

Key Points

- Family dynamics impact the roles we play, even after leaving our childhood home.

- One symptom of harmful family dynamics is having a pessimistic and harmful internal monologue.

- Breaking down family dynamics requires attention and effort.

- Breaking down family dynamics has many benefits and helps you live a freer and more authentic life.

Reflective Questions

- How do you think family dynamics impact you today?

_____
_____
_____
_____
_____

- What is your internal monologue like? Are you normally pessimistic with yourself or optimistic?

_____
_____
_____
_____
_____

- Do you want to break down harmful family dynamics?

_____
_____
_____
_____
_____

- How will you break down harmful family dynamics?

_____
_____
_____
_____
_____

- What positive outcomes are you looking forward to when you start living authentically?

_____
_____
_____
_____
_____

Action Plan

- Understand how family dynamics impact you today.

_____
_____
_____
_____
_____

- Reflect on which family dynamics are harmful.

_____
_____
_____
_____
_____

- Release these harmful family dynamics.

_____
_____
_____
_____
_____

- Celebrate the improvements you see in your life.

_____
_____

- Be patient with yourself. Progress is not always linear.

Chapter 10 – How to Identify Emotionally Mature People

The tenth and final chapter of the book is titled "How to Identify Emotionally Mature People." People with emotionally immature parents don't often see a relationship as fulfilling. Because their parents did not meet their emotional needs, these people don't believe that an adult relationship will meet their needs.

Finding Emotionally Mature People

Finding fulfilling adult relationships can be difficult. As John Bowlby noted in his 1979 research, humans have a primitive instinct that equates familiarity with safety. If your parents were emotionally immature, **you have a higher tendency to pursue (or tolerate) emotionally immature people** in your life. To prevent this from happening, it is essential that you can **recognize people who are emotionally mature**. Some common characteristics of emotionally mature people include:

- They are realistic

- They are reliable

- They are logical even when emotions are high.

- They are consistent.

- They are reciprocal.

- They respect boundaries

- They can compromise.

- They are even-keeled and don't have emotional outbursts

- They will change their minds when necessary.

- They tell the truth.

- They apologize when they make mistakes.

- They work to repair relationships.

- They are responsive.

- They are empathetic.

- They make you feel safe.

- You enjoy being around them.

- They are comfortable giving and receiving support.

- They self-reflect and make changes when necessary.

- They can be humorous.

- You enjoy being around them.

After covering these common traits of emotionally mature people, the author has some advice for meeting people online. First, it's important to remember that some people have better writing skills than others. However, everyone's written communication reveals something about the person. The most important thing to note when talking to someone online is the pace of the conversation. If they **respect our boundaries and the communication is reciprocal**, you've probably found an emotionally mature individual.

To further help you gauge a person's emotional maturity, the other details a helpful exercise. In this assessment, pick someone in your life and check off all the boxes that are true about them.

Assessing Emotional Maturity Exercise

- They accept reality rather than fight it.

- They allow themselves to feel without letting their emotions control them.

- They are consistent and reliable.

- Not everything is personal to them.

- They treat boundaries with respect.

- They are reciprocal.

- They do not lie.

- They can compromise.

- They apologize and work to repair the relationship.

- They are empathetic.

- You feel safe, seen, and understood when around them.

- They self-reflect.

- You enjoy being around them.

It may be necessary to build new relationship habits to create relationships with emotionally mature people. The author includes some final exercises to help you build these healthier relationship habits.

Building Healthy Relationship Habits Exercises

1. Be willing to ask for help.

   - Remind yourself that most people like helping others.

   - When asking for help, use clear communication to explain your feelings and reasonings.

2. Be authentic, regardless of what others think.

   - Don't try to control how others perceive you.

   - Set healthy boundaries.

   - Stand up for your values and beliefs.

3. Sustain and appreciate emotional connections.

   - Keep in touch with the people who are there for you.

   - You deserve love and friendship.

- Don't let emotions control your actions.

4. Be realistic with yourself.

    - Apologies for your mistakes, but remember that mistakes are inevitable.

    - Do not try to guess what others want. Their emotions are their responsibility.

    - Take care of your mental and physical health.

5. Use clear communication and focus on the outcomes you want.

    - Don't expect people to know your needs. Communicate them.

    - Understand your own emotions.

    - Be thoughtful to others, but expect them to treat you with thoughtfulness too.

After this final exercise, the book ends with a brief epilogue. In this epilogue, the author reminds readers that it is important to **understand your childhood** and its impact on you today. Through this understanding, you can begin to **break down the fantasies, role-self, and harmful family dynamics that negatively impact you**. While this process can be difficult, going through this process of self-discovery allows you to live a more authentic life and surround yourself with emotionally mature people.

Key Points

- It can be difficult to build relationships with emotionally mature people. This is because we often fall into the familiar.

- To build healthy relationships, you must learn to identify emotionally mature people.

- You also need to take responsibility for your own role in relationships and work to build better habits.

- This is a lot of work. But the rewards are well worth the effort.

Reflective Questions

- Do you think you stay in relationships with emotionally immature people?

_____
_____
_____
_____
_____

- According to the Assessing Emotional Maturity exercise, are the people in your life emotionally mature?

_____
_____
_____
_____
_____

- What is the most important thing to remember when meeting someone online?

_____

_____

_____

_____

_____

- What exercises will you use to build healthy relationships?

_____

_____

_____

_____

_____

Action Plan

- Don't fall into the mistake of chasing emotionally immature relationships because they are familiar.

_____

_____

_____

_____

_____

- Take the Assessing Emotional Maturity exercise for the people in your life.

_____

_____

_____

_____

_____

- Think about the role you play in your relationships. Are you emotionally mature?

_____

_____

_____

_____

_____

- Pick a few of the Building Healthy Relationship Habits Exercises to incorporate into your life.

_____

_____

_____

_____

_____

Background Information About *Adult Children of Emotionally Immature Parents*

Adult Children of Emotionally Immature Parents by Gibson was published in June 2015. The book addresses the concept of emotional neglect and how being emotionally neglected can have a lifelong impact. This concept is explored further in the ten chapters of the book. The first chapter addresses the emotional loneliness people with emotionally immature parents often feel. The next two chapters dive into the characteristics of emotionally immature people and common relationship problems. The fourth chapter discusses the four types of emotionally immature parents and how to identify them. The fifth chapter reveals how children with emotionally immature parents can lose their sense of self. In the next chapter, the author describes two personality types for dealing with emotional loneliness and provides exercises for identifying your type. In chapter seven, the author describes the breakdown that can happen through living un-authentically. Chapter eight introduces the maturity awareness approach, a way of relating to people based on their emotional level. The second to last chapter details the freedom and relief one can find after living authentically. Lastly, the tenth chapter advises finding emotionally mature people and building healthy relationships.

Through reading the book, the author wants readers to be able to identify emotionally immature people and understand how their childhood continues to affect their life. Readers will also learn how to communicate with emotionally immature people while finding emotionally mature individuals and building relationships with them.

Background Information About Lindsay C. Gibson

The author, Lindsay C. Gibson, is a clinical psychologist with a doctorate in psychology. She specializes in individual psychotherapy for people who have emotionally immature parents. In addition to her book *Adult Children of Emotionally Immature Parents*, she has also written *Who You Were Meant to Be*. Additionally, she has a monthly column in the Tidewater Women magazine, a magazine devoted to the well-being of women. In addition to her private practice and writing endeavors, she has been an adjunct assistant professor of graduate psychology for two different colleges. These schools are the College of William and Mary and Old Dominion University. She currently lives in Virginia Beach, Virginia, close to her practice.

List of Exercises

Adult Children of Emotionally Immature Parents includes a variety of exercises to help people identify emotional maturity (and immaturity), live more authentically, and build healthier relationships. A complete list of the exercises and the associated chapter can be found below as a reference guide.

- Emotional Immaturity Exercise - Chapter 2

- Childhood Difficulties Exercise - Chapter 3

- Parent Type Exercise - Chapter 4

- Healing Fantasy and Role-Self Exercise - Chapter 5

- Internalizer/Externalizer Assessment - Chapter 5

- True Self and Role-Self Exercise - Chapter 7

- Assessing Emotional Maturity Exercise - Chapter 10

- Building Healthy Relationship Habits Exercises - Chapter 10

Discussion Questions

1. Before reading the book, how would you have defined emotional immaturity and emotional maturity?

2. Were your original ideas about emotional maturity accurate, or did you learn something new from this book?

3. Before reading this book, would you have considered your parents emotionally immature? Has your answer changed after reading this book?

4. Do you think your parent's parents were emotionally immature? If so, do you think that affected how they raised you?

5. Do you think your childhood continues to affect you today? If so, what about your childhood still affects you?

6. Did you take the internalizer vs. externalizer assessment? If so, were you surprised by the results?

7. Think through the people in your life. How many of them are emotionally immature? How many are emotionally mature?

8. What outcomes do you have for the relationships in your life?

9. Did the book make you question or reevaluate any of the relationships in your life?

10. If you have children, did the book change anything about how you plan on raising them?

11. Do you consider yourself emotionally mature? If not, do you want to be emotionally mature?

12. To grow your emotional maturity, what exercises from the book will you use?

13. Are you living an authentic life? If not, do you want to?

14. What do you need to change if you want to live an authentic life? How are you going to change those things?

More books from Smart Reads

Summary of the Case for Keto by Gary Taubes

Summary of Eat Smarter by Shawn Stevenson

Summary of 4 Hour Body by Tim Ferriss

Summary of Dr. Gundry's Diet Evolution by Dr. Steven
      Gundry

Summary of Exercised by David E. Lieberman

Summary of End Your Carb Confusion by Eric C. Westman
      with Amy Berger

Summary of Fast This Way by Dave Asprey

Summary of Dr. Kellyann's Bone Broth Diet by Dr. Kellyann
      Petrucci

Summary of Permission to Feel by Dr. Marc Brackett

Summary of Unwinding Anxiety by Judson Brewer

Summary of Set Boundaries, Find Peace by Nedra Glover
      Tawwab

Summary of The Complete Guide to Fasting by Jason Fung
      with Jimmy Moore

Summary of The Diabetes Code by Jason Fung

Summary of The Obesity Code by Jason Fung

Summary of A Radical Awakening by Dr. Shefali Tsabary

Summary of Influence, New and Expanded by Robert B.
      Cialdini

Summary of Think Again by Adam Grant

Summary of How to do the Work by Dr. Nicole LePera

Summary of COVID-19: The Great Reset by Steven E.
      Koonin

Summary of Unsettled: What Climate Science Tells Us,
      What It Doesn't, and Why It Matters by Steven E.
      Koonin

Summary of What Happened to You? by Oprah Winfrey
      and Dr. Bruce Perry

Summary of Breath: The New Science of a Lost Art By
James Nestor
Workbook for What Happened to You? By Oprah Winfrey
and Dr. Bruce Perry
Workbook for Limitless By Jim Kwik
Workbook for The Body Keeps the Score By Dr. Bessel van
der Kolk
Workbook for Atlas of the Heart By Brené Brown
Workbook for Fast Like a Girl By Dr. Mindy Pelz
Workbook for The Tools By Phil Stutz and Barry Michels
Workbook for Glucose Revolution By Jessie Inchauspe
Workbook for Forgiving What You Can't Forget by Lysa
TerKeurst

Thank You

Hope you've enjoyed your reading experience.

We here at Smart Reads will always strive to deliver to you the highest quality guides.

So I'd like to thank you for supporting us and reading until the very end.

Before you go, would you mind leaving us a review on Amazon?

It will mean a lot to us and support us creating high quality guides for you in the future.

Thanks once again!

Warmly yours,

The Smart Reads Team

Download Your Free Gift

As a way to say "Thank You" for being a fan of our series,
I've included a free gift for you:

Brain Health: How to Nurture and Nourish Your Brain For
Top Performance

Go to www.smart-reads.com to get your
FREE book.

The Smart Reads Team

Made in the USA
Las Vegas, NV
10 March 2024

86925113R00056